Go the Extra Mile

Workbook 4

Go the Extra Mile

Workbook 4

CREDITS:

VP, Product Development:	**Matt Gambino**
Production Editor:	**Genevieve McDermott**
Production Artists:	**Nicole Phillips and Rich Lehl**
Advisor:	**Margery Steinberg, Ph.D.**
Cartoonist:	**James McFarlane**

Based on materials by Robert Taggart, Ph.D., Remediation & Training Institute
Editorial services provided by Watershed Books

COPYRIGHT © 2006 Axzo Press. All Rights Reserved..

No part of this work may be reproduced, transcribed, or used in any form or by any means—graphic, electronic, or mechanical, including photocopying, recording, taping, Web distribution, or information storage and retrieval systems—without the prior written permission of the publisher.

For more, go to **www.axzopress.com**

Trademarks

Crisp Series is a trademark of Axzo Press.

Some of the product names and company names used in this book have been used for identification purposes only and may be trademarks or registered trademarks of their respective manufacturers and sellers.

Disclaimer

We reserve the right to revise this publication and make changes from time to time in its content without notice.

ISBN 10: 1-4239-5070-4
ISBN 13: 978-1-4239-5070-7
Library of Congress Catalog Card Number 98-93600
Printed in the United States of America
4 5 6 11 10

Learning Objectives for

GO THE EXTRA MILE

The learning objectives for *Go the Extra Mile* are listed below. They have been developed to guide the user to the core issues covered in this book.

The objectives of this book are to help the user:

1) Maintain key information on customers

2) Conduct customer follow-up

3) Provide the customer with a personalized business card

4) Schedule personal appointments with shoppers; select merchandise in advance

Preface

Welcome to the *Crisp Retailing Smarts Series,* designed specifically for the retail sales associate. This series is based on skill standards developed by a team of industry practitioners and educators under the leadership of the National Retail Federation, the world's largest retail association.

The topics covered in these workbooks reflect what employers across the country agree is needed to succeed and grow in a retail career, regardless of the size or nature of the enterprise. The *Crisp Retailing Smarts Series* sets a new standard for industry-driven learning that leads to productive and measurable results and helps prepare candidates for rewarding careers in retail and other service industries.

The skill standards followed here have been developed for the professional sales associate for several reasons:

➤ The majority of North American workers initially enter the workforce through a job in the retail industry. Many choose to make retailing a lifelong career, adding new skills as they progress.

➤ The skills required for success in these entry-level positions are the same skills that will help workers succeed throughout their lives, both personally and professionally, whether in the retail industry or some other field of work or profession.

➤ In our current service-oriented and global economy, organizations must attract and retain a dedicated, competitive workforce. Skills are a key attribute when selecting these workers.

As you use these materials, take advantage of the exercises and self-assessments that will help you better understand the skills and techniques being explained. Studies show that adults retain new skills more effectively if they apply them immediately to their own experiences. After you have completed the reading and activities in each section, look for opportunities to put the lessons into practice. Then use the *Learning Checklist* in the back of the book to record your progress and successes.

We are proud to help the retailing industry pioneer the development of skill standards and raise expectations for a committed and competitive workforce. And we are proud that learners like yourself are taking your future into your own hands and mastering the skills that will bring you success and recognition in your chosen profession.

Tracy Mullin

Tracy Mullin
President and CEO
National Retail Federation

Add the Finishing Touches to Your Customer Service

Whether you are just preparing for your first job in retail or you are a seasoned sales associate, there are always additional skills to discover and new techniques to practice. A few of the more advanced customer service skills have been collected in this workbook to get you started on your journey to the next level in your profession.

If you have shopped in stores that practice any of these techniques, you are already familiar with the impact they can have on customers. When a sales associate calls you to make sure you are satisfied with your purchase, it makes you feel important. When you receive a handwritten note thanking you for your business, you know that store appreciates you.

When a sales associate hands you a business card and encourages you to return, you realize someone is always there to help you. When you return to a store and the associate remembers your name, you know you will receive personal attention once again. This is the kind of shopping experience we'd all like to have, especially when we're pressed for time, not finding the items we need, or simply looking for the personalized customer service that makes shopping more enjoyable.

Table of Contents

P A R T 1

Conduct Customer Follow-Up

Conduct Customer Follow-Up

Customer follow-up can occur in a number of ways, and for a variety of reasons. The important thing is to use a method suited to the customer and the situation. In this case, one size does not fit all! Here are a few examples of matching the follow-up method and message to the customer and purchase:

1. Telephone message

"Mr. Stavros, this is Angela at The Well Heeled and I just wanted to make sure your boots arrived. Our records show they were shipped last Friday. If you have not received them by now, or if you have any concerns about your order please call me at.... If everything is to your satisfaction, no need to call back. Thank you for the opportunity to serve you and I hope you'll come see me next time you need shoes."

2. Thank-you card

"Dear Mrs. Rhodes, I certainly enjoyed helping you select a garden bench for your yard and I hope you are enjoying your morning coffee among the many birds that you mentioned visit your garden. Please come see us again at Gracious Gardens—we loved hearing about your planting adventures. Sincerely, Doug Harper."

3. E-mail

"Dear Mrs. Jenks, I just wanted to check in to verify that your new computer desk fit the space you had in mind. Hopefully you are enjoying the new workspace as you read this. If you have further needs for your home office, please call me. Thank you, Glenn Yoshida."

Follow-Up Etiquette

In addition to matching your method and message to your customers and their purchases, there are some other things you should consider in planning your follow-up. The first, of course, is whether you should follow up at all!

To follow up or not... Not every purchase requires a follow-up. You needn't call a customer who just bought a ninety-cent pen to see if he's happy with it. On the other hand, if the customer who bought the pen told you he was testing it out to see if he was going to order a large quantity for his office, it would make sense to follow up with him.

Certain types of merchandise—appliances or computers, for example—are costly and can be damaged during delivery. After such a purchase, it is customary for the sales associate to contact the customer to make sure the merchandise was received in good condition—*after* the scheduled delivery date, not before.

You may also want to ask the customer if the store's delivery people were courteous and careful. Their satisfactory performance is also part of what you're selling the customer.

Phone savvy... Exercise good judgment when conducting telephone follow-up. Not every customer will appreciate one more phone call in his or her busy day, so be sure that the customer's purchase warrants phone follow-up. If it does, consider the most appropriate time and place for that call.

For example, you may have noticed that telemarketers tend to call at dinnertime because they know people are likely to be home. Many customers resent such an interruption (unless they have specifically asked you to call at night).

It might be better to call during the day, leaving a voice message if necessary. In most cases it is acceptable to leave a message such as the following:

> **Sales Associate:** "This is Taylor, from the Computer Store, and I just wanted to make sure your PC was delivered. I enjoyed helping you select a workstation for your son. No need to return this call if everything is okay, but please call me at 123-4567 if you have any problems with your computer or software or if I can be of further service."

This leaves the customer in control and does not place an unnecessary burden on him to call you back.

Keep it professional…Sending an occasional postcard to your best customers is one very effective—and unobtrusive—way to maintain your relationship with them. While you want to personalize your notes by writing them by hand, you don't want to get personal in a way that would make your customer uncomfortable or that would seem inappropriate. For instance, you can write Rita Lamarr that you hope the wedding shoes she purchased were comfortable during her ceremony. But you don't want to ask her if she had too much champagne at the reception!

Tip: *Be sensitive about using postcards that others may read. For example, if you are following up on a gift purchase, enclose your note in an envelope.*

Staying in Touch

Make it pleasurable…The last thing in the world you want to do is alienate your best customers by making a pest out of yourself with too many cards and calls. Staying in touch with customers should be a pleasant, reassuring experience for the customer. A note to a customer immediately following a purchase is acceptable. So are occasional contacts that provide your customer with information she will value—a sale, an in-store promotional event, etc. However, it does not mean camping on the customer's doorstep, leaving a note on the customer's windshield, or visiting the customer at her place of work.

In their best interests…Most stores advertise special sales or other promotional events. But customers do not always pay attention to these ads. Customers often appreciate receiving a postcard that informs them of key events, tells them about no-interest charges on store accounts during Christmas, or reminds them of the birthday discount your store offers. It makes customers feel special and shows them that you are looking out for their best interests. A handwritten note from you may also give them that extra incentive to come in.

Valuable contacts…This is where knowing your customers and referring to your client records come in handy. Use your client record system to note items your customer asks for and is interested in—even if you are unable to provide them at the moment. The store may get the merchandise in the future, or you may find some alternative merchandise that would suit the customer's needs. Then you can contact the customer. Even if he no longer needs the item, the customer usually appreciates that "you remembered."

WHEN TO FOLLOW UP

Following are a few situations that warrant follow-up with a customer, including one example of the type of follow-up that might be appropriate. For the remaining situations, write in your own ideas of what follow-up might be appropriate.

<u>SITUATION</u>	<u>FOLLOW-UP</u>
Your customer comes in every few months to see if you have any new neckties from his favorite designer.	Write him a note to let him know that you are expecting a new shipment in a week. Offer to hold some for him if he calls you with color preferences.
1. Your customer has purchased an entertainment center and asked to have it delivered and set up in her home.	
2. A customer recently returned a golf bag because it did not have all the features he wanted. You have just found one in your catalog that might fit his needs.	
3. The customer has been waiting for some specific new books to become available. They have finally arrived.	
4. A customer has been in several times to look at wallpaper and has taken samples home but can't decide. You just found out one of your suppliers is sponsoring a wallpaper clinic, to be conducted by a noted decorator.	

Compare your answers to the suggestions in the Appendix.

P A R T 2

Use Business
Cards Artfully

Use Business Cards Artfully

Today, many people exchange business cards when making introductions. This is an effective and efficient way to share basic information such as your name, phone number, and job title. If your company provides business cards, you can use them to suggest to customers that they contact you personally for future needs. If your company does not provide business cards, you can write this information on the sales receipt, special order form, or note card. Use the following tips to make this exchange most effective.

The power of a card... Your business card not only tells the customer who you are, it also tells the customer that you are serious about your work. While not all stores provide sales associates cards with their own names printed on them, most have store business cards on which you can write your name, department, telephone extension or other information needed by the customer. Such additional information might include:

➤ Tips for the use and care of a purchase

➤ Item ordered and date when a special request should be fulfilled

➤ Name and location of a recommended repair shop or other service

➤ Directions to the warehouse for a pickup

➤ Reminder of an upcoming sale or other promotional event

When you give a customer your card, make certain you write down the hours the store is open, and the times during the week when you work. You may also be able to offer an e-mail address or a pager number that will give customers quicker, easier access to you. By doing this, you emphasize your interest in continuing to be of service.

If your store does not provide business cards...

➤ Write your name and other information on the sales receipt.

➤ Write a quick thank-you note on store stationery and staple it to the receipt.

➤ Write "Hope to see you at our Anniversary Sale" on a sale flyer or postcard, sign your name, and put it in the bag with the purchased item.

➤ Write "Call me if you have any questions" on the assembly instructions and add your name and phone number.

➤ Make your own business cards!

Business Cards for Under $20

If your store does not provide business cards for you to use, one option is to make your own! Just check with your employer first to make sure this does not violate any company rules.

Having a personal business card is a great way to say "I am dedicated to serving my customers." Here are just a few ideas for creating your own cards that will cost you less than $20 for as many as 250 cards.

Business Card Stationery

You can buy paper that is already perforated so you can cut or tear it into the size of business cards. The perforations are very fine, so the result is a smooth-edged card. This paper also has colored designs already printed on it, so you get an attractive, eye-catching card. The paper costs less than $15 at stationery, paper, or office supply stores.

The paper is designed for use in computer printers, so you can make them on your home or school computer or ask a friend to make them for you. Most public libraries now have computers and printers which you can schedule to use free of charge.

Quick Print Shops

Small, local shops specializing in rapid, inexpensive printing services are a growing business. You can find at least one of these even in small communities; in large cities there seems to be one on almost every block. These shops offer special deals to print business cards for as little as $20. For this price, you can have your name, address, phone number, job title, even a slogan, printed in black ink on white card stock. Many also allow you to include a graphic from the shop's selection of clip art, for no extra charge. Clip art is small drawings, icons, or other images that are computer-ready and easy to add to any computer-generated document. You can select an image that reflects the kind of product or service you sell or one that reflects your personal values about customer service.

**Simple type created
on a computer or by
quick print shop**

Clip art

Pre-printed border

Angela Flowers

12201 S. Broad St., Honolulu, HI 96815
Phone (808) 884-4411 • Fax (808) 884-4412

Paper with pre-printed image

CJ PARTY SUPPLY

Jody Plemel
Sales Associate

123 E. Lander, Watertown, MA
Ph: 926-3344 / fax: 926-3445

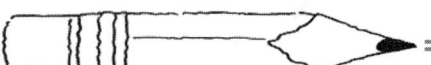

DESIGN YOUR OWN BUSINESS CARDS

Using inspiration from the examples on the previous pages, design a business card you could use in your job. If you are not currently working in a retail position, imagine the ideal job for you and design a card for that.

Your card should have the following information on it:

➤ Your name and job title

➤ Your company's name (optional)

➤ Address and phone number

➤ A slogan, either for your store or for you personally

Include an image—a border design, a logo, illustration, or cartoon, that would tell your customers something about you or about the products or services you sell.

Hint: look through magazines, the telephone directory, and the newspaper for ideas.

CONTINUED

CONTINUED

Follow the "Rules" of Business Card Etiquette

Follow the "Rules" of Business Card Etiquette

First time's the charm…If possible, make sure the customer has your business card before he leaves your store for the first time. However, don't "lead with your card." Help the customer find what she is looking for, complete the transaction if one results, and then offer your card and future services. Or you may simply attach your card to the sales receipt and encourage your new customer to call if you can help her again.

You can also offer your card to a customer who is just considering an item and wants a day or two to make a decision. That card is your customer's reminder that when he is ready to buy, you're ready to serve him.

Keep it clean…Your business card is a reflection on you, so make sure it projects a professional image. Never give a customer a card that has been folded, has fingerprints or lipstick smudges, or has handwritten notes on it that are not specifically intended for that customer. Keep an adequate supply on hand, preferably in a card holder or box where they will stay clean.

Staying in touch…Any time you send a note to a customer, whether it's a thank you note or a notice of a forthcoming sale, be sure to enclose your card. It can have the same power as your signature in terms of reminding your customer of the special service you deliver. It also says "Don't forget to ask for me again."

Tip: Unless customers ask for several, offer them just one of your business cards. If you hand them more than one card, they might think you're asking them to distribute your cards to other potential customers. You want to keep the emphasis on person-to-person contact.

Accepting the Customer's Business Card

You first…A good rule of thumb is never to ask for a customer's business card unless you've offered your own card first. And keep in mind that many customers will not have business cards; others may not be comfortable using them for personal business.

Some reasons that you might ask for business cards, or simply customer contact information, include:

➤ A customer is asking about performance of a product; you have offered to research it.

➤ You mention an upcoming sale and the customer shows interest; you offer to remind her.

➤ The customer is disappointed that you are out of a specific item; you offer to call him when a new shipment arrives.

➤ You cannot solve a customer's problem, but you offer to give it further thought and call her back if you think of something.

➤ An item needs to be altered or customized; you promise to contact the customer when it is ready for pickup.

In other words, if your reason for requesting a card has direct benefit to the customer, then go ahead and ask. But don't just randomly collect business cards to create a potential client list. The customer may see this as pushy or a threat to his privacy. Some experts on business manners even advise that if the person you're helping holds a significant business position (you happen to know she's president of the bank across the street), you should *always* wait for the customer to offer her card, rather than ask for it.

Treat the gesture with respect…When a customer does give you her business card, don't just shove it in your pocket. Look it over with interest. At least use the person's name to indicate you've read it ("Ms. Jones," unless she says "Call me Susan"). You might also add, "Oh, we do business with your bank" or "How was your commute from downtown this evening?" If nothing else, you could compliment the logo or other design element. The point is, you're taking time to show that you are honored to receive the card and you're paying attention to what it tells you about the customer. Also consider that if you put the card in your purse or wallet, the customer may worry you have personal intentions. It would be better to place it in a card file, daily planner, or your client record system.

Make the card count…If a customer hands you a business card, use it as a reference card. Jot down a few notes about the customer and his preferences, special requests, or other information that will help you serve him later. If you're keeping a client record, as we suggest next, you can transfer those notes to it later. That way, you can contact the customer if something comes in that might interest him.

Tip: *If a customer's business card includes a pager number or e-mail address, be sure to ask if it is okay to use these methods for contacting him.*

THE ART OF THE CARD EXCHANGE

Which of the following examples follow the proper etiquette for requesting or offering business cards? Check (✓) only those which you feel are acceptable.

❑ **Sales Associate:** "I've enjoyed helping you select a wedding gift for your nephew, Mrs. Allen. Here is my business card in case I can be of any further assistance. Feel free to call me directly if you have any questions or special requests. Thank you, and enjoy the wedding!"

❑ **Sales Associate:** "Well, if you change your mind and do want some help, here's my card. Just tell the other sales people that I am already helping you."

❑ **Sales Associate:** "I'm glad I was able to help you find what you needed today. Here are a few of my cards—be sure and tell your friends and family about me."

❑ **Sales Associate:** "I'm sorry we don't carry that brand, but I think you'd be just as happy with the new model we have on order. If you have a business card, I could call you when it comes in."

❑ **Sales Associate:** "I agree you should give this some more thought if it is not exactly what you had in mind. Here is my card in case you think of any additional questions. In the meantime, if you'd like for me to keep an eye out as we get new shipments, I'd be happy to take your number and call you if I spot anything closer to your description."

❑ **Sales Associate:** "We don't have business cards here, but if you'll give me yours I will call you whenever something interesting comes in."

❑ **Sales Associate:** "I'm sorry I don't have a personalized business card to give you, but I've put my name, phone number, and the hours you can reach me on your sales slip—don't hesitate to call me if you have any questions about your new purchase."

Compare your answers to those in the Appendix.

P A R T 4

Maintain Key Information on Customers

Maintain Key Information on Customers

Few salespeople can instantly recall everything they need to know about a customer when he walks back into a store—even if he's a frequent shopper. If you want to succeed in offering great personal service to customers, you will rely on maintaining a record of needs, preferences, and other information that customers willingly share with you.

Keeping a client record... This will be your method for recording information about customers. You may want to start with friends and family members who may become your frequent customers. This record system will contain basic information that allows you to stay in touch with your customers. It will also contain specific information that helps you to deliver personalized assistance, such as notifying your customer when you see a new item come into the store that might be of interest to her. Let's say you have a customer who buys large quantities of a high-priced brand of panty hose twice a year. You will become her favorite sales associate, someone she depends upon, when you call her, send her a postcard, or e-mail her to let her know when there's a 20 percent discount on this brand.

Your client record system may be a notepad, a computer file, a card file, a folder, or a simple three-ring binder with a separate page for each customer. Use the type of recording system that works best for you. The important thing is to collect information and keep it up-to-date.

SAMPLE CLIENT RECORD

Office Objects, Inc.
"we make your business our business"

Sales Associate: Kim

Customer name: Mr. Flanders

Work phone: 327-2375   **FAX:** 327-2300

Company Name: Tech Trainers

Mailing Address: 100 Union St. Suite 400

Fairhaven, CT 08118

Type of Business: Business Training

Special Requests:

3/5/97	Looking for 10 bin paper organizer for document storage, white, no larger than 3' H x 4' W
4/3/97	Found in Spring '97 catalog, item # 557-9805, $59.99. Called customer and ordered.
12/11/97	bought new MP5000 printer and one extra cartridge
2/15/98	ordered additional cartridge; high volume use — notify of cartridge specials

Special Services:

4/18/97	Had paper bin delivered and assembled.
2/15/98	Placed on mailing list for sale notification.

What to record…You can begin by recording information about potential customers—friends and family, even people who come into your store but don't buy anything. If they are looking for a specific item but don't find it, make a note about their request in case you can help them later. Record any purchases your customers make so you can begin to understand their shopping habits. In addition, use this record to keep track of your follow-up activities. Include notes about any sale notices, coupons, thank you cards, promotional announcements, invitations to demonstrations or workshops, etc., that you've sent to each customer. If you know certain customers have responded to your special notices, make a note of that as well. You will remember to include them in future special activities. Some professional sales associates try to recognize special dates in the lives of their customers, such as birthdays and anniversaries, with a card or special offering.

Basic ingredients…Your client records should contain the following basic information for each customer:

➤ Name

➤ Address

➤ Telephone

➤ Occupation (or hobbies, collections, activities, projects, or other interests that influence buying preferences)

Next, add information that will help you to maintain a current profile of the customer's personal preferences and needs. For example:

➤ Date and type of first purchase or contact. What was the customer shopping for? Did he or she buy anything?

➤ Preferences or specifications. Are there size variables by brand name or type of item? Color or style preferences? Label or brand-name preferences?

➤ Special considerations. Is your customer allergic to certain fibers? Does she travel a lot? Does he work the night shift?

➤ Does your customer prefer to have goods delivered? Assembled? Serviced regularly?

Reviewing to discover opportunities…You will want to review the information in your client records regularly. New opportunities may suddenly arise. For instance, your notes say that John Nesbitt has been looking for a recliner that doesn't look like a recliner. One has just arrived in your department. This is your opportunity to shine as the most thoughtful sales associate he's ever encountered. You may also have new ideas of ways to help customer Della Moore improve the efficiency of the home office she is setting up—you've just found a desktop shelving system that has everything!

> ❝ *The only person who behaves sensibly is my tailor. He takes new measurements every time he sees me. All the rest go on with their old measurements.*❞

–**George Bernard Shaw, English playwright and author**

Keep it new…As you've probably guessed, your collection of customer information is a "living" record. Customers' preferences, needs, sizes, etc., may change considerably over time. Just as you keep up with friends and family, it will be vital for you to keep up with your return customers. Record every new bit of information you receive—whether it's that Sally Mason has moved from the city to the suburbs, Joe Pascal is now self-employed instead of a corporate guy, or Maria Martinez has decided she never wants to wear black again.

Keep it confidential…Privacy is important to everyone. As a sales associate, you may learn some very personal things about your customers. Be careful about what you say to others. Even such information as dress size or birth date is very personal. Never leave your client records on the counter. Check with your manager to see what the store policy is about storing this information; perhaps a locked cabinet or individual locker can be provided.

It is not up to you to decide what information about the customer should or should not be private. Keep all information that you gather about your customers confidential. Do not share customer information with anyone—even co-workers— without the customer's knowledge and permission. A customer will have more confidence in you if you respect his privacy. Types of confidential information that you may learn and should never share without the customer's permission:

➤ Home address and phone number

➤ Credit card numbers

➤ Times the customer is or is not home to accept a delivery

➤ Sizes

➤ Birth date

➤ Occupation or place of business

CREATING A CLIENT RECORD

Using this template, begin creating a client record by noting as much information as you can about one of your customers.

If you are not currently working as a sales associate, practice creating a client record by gathering information about someone you like to shop for—perhaps someone for whom you buy birthday, holiday, and special occasion gifts.

confidential
Client Profile

Name: _____

Address: _____ Phone: _____

City/State/Zip: _____ Birthday: _____

Work: _____ Title: _____

Email: _____ Fax: _____

Contact Restrictions/Requests: _____

Personal Profile (preferences, sizes, etc.): _____

Buying History: _____

Recent Requests/Status: _____

*Additional copies of this form are included in the back of this workbook.
Use them to begin creating your client record system.*

Offer Personal

Shopper Services

Offer Personal Shopper Services

One of the most satisfying and creative ways of serving a customer is when you act as a personal shopper. Not only does this give you some interesting challenges in terms of testing what you know about your customer's needs and preferences, but it also offers you and the store a special opportunity to be *the* store, *the* sales associate that knows how to give personalized customer service!

Creating Confidence

When you act as a personal shopper, the ability to understand the customer's needs is absolutely essential. As you learned earlier in this book, the successful sales associate learns by observing, asking skillful questions, and paying attention to customer clues. You may not always have an established relationship with someone who enlists you as a personal shopper. But that customer will expect you to come up with options that suit her personally. If you don't, then you have wasted the valuable time she was trying to save by having you make selections for her. Your best tools for this job are *listening* carefully to what she says, *writing* yourself some notes so you don't forget, and then *selecting* only items that fit her interests.

Tune in to the customer…A customer you have just met has asked you to pick out some clothes for her tropical vacation. Rather than search through the racks herself, she has asked you to find the best choices for her needs. Then she'll come by at a scheduled time to make the final selection. If this was a return customer, you would probably have notes in your client record about her likes and dislikes—colors, size, style, brands, etc. Since you have just met this customer, you'll need to remember everything you observed and heard her say, such as:

> **Customer:** "I don't like skimpy or see-through resortwear. And I'm not crazy about pastel colors. I like clothes that are comfortable yet elegant."
>
> **What You Know:** (1) probably prefers conservative lengths in skirts and shorts; (2) nothing transparent or gauzy; (3) pick classic neutral or dramatic seasonal colors; (4) simple lines and coordinated sets for an elegant look—possibly elastic waistbands, loose-fitting styles.

You might ask a few questions to clarify the color and style issues, and you should probably ask her what kind of activities she'll be participating in—such as sports, formal dinners, or just relaxing by the water. Most customers won't be upset if you aren't 100-percent successful in meeting all their needs—if you come close, they'll appreciate your efforts. But if you're way off base, they'll lose confidence in you.

Scheduling Appointments

Over time, you will collect valuable information from your return customers not only about their merchandise preferences, but about items they're hoping you will eventually have in stock. For example, you may have a customer who collects imported crystal figurines. She appreciates knowing when each new shipment arrives, since the quantities are limited and she's a collector. You know that you should contact this customer immediately when new shipments of the figurines arrive. You also reserve pieces for the customer that you feel will be good additions to her collection.

Schedule individual appointments for such customers. That way, you can attend to each customer according to his or her needs.

Keep your appointment schedule in a book or some portable format, so you can carry it with you. That will help you prevent scheduling conflicts, in both your personal and professional life. By keeping your appointment book with you, you can also contact customers if an emergency comes up and you have to reschedule.

Write down the name and telephone number of the customer and the time and purpose of the appointment. If the customer is shopping for a particular item, write down what it is and all the important details. The day before the appointment, call to confirm the date and time.

Accommodations count…Go in a little early or stay a little later if that is what is needed to meet your customer's needs—and if your store policy allows this. Or trade hours with a co-worker who is working on a day your customer wants to shop. The point here is that a special effort on your part may be well worth your while—not just for one sale, but for the many that will likely follow.

Scheduling Personal Shopper Appointments

Here are some situations where you might want to schedule an appointment with a customer:

➤ To show your customer items you've pre-selected, at her request

➤ You have a special customer who likes undivided attention, even when she is "just looking"

➤ Your customer has a busy schedule and is always in a hurry

➤ A customer relies on you to help him select all of his gift purchases around certain holidays and family events

---

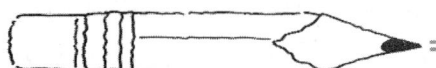

YOUR OWN PERSONAL SHOPPER

Personal shoppers have to be very tuned-in to what their customers are looking for. To increase your ability to tune in to customer requests, pretend that you are planning a dream vacation and need some help getting prepared. This vacation should be designed around your interests—a pampered week at a spa, an outdoor adventure, a month trekking around a foreign country, or a visit to a sports-oriented resort—you pick!

Now make a list of all the things you'll need to buy and write down what your personal shopper will need to know in order to select just the right items for you.

Be specific—this sales associate has never met you before. For instance, you may need to provide guidance on things like brands, quality, colors, sizes, how many, etc.

Your dream vacation:

_____

_____

_____

_____

_____

_____

What you need from your personal shopper:

_____

_____

_____

_____

_____

_____

_____

_____

A P P E N D I X

Roundup: Go the Extra Mile

In this workbook, you have learned the value of going the extra mile for your customers. You have also read about some ways that you can go that extra distance that sets you apart from the competition. When customers begin to rely on your knowledge and appreciate your personalized attention, they may become clients for life. They may even seek you out if you change jobs, knowing that they can trust you to treat them well.

The list that follows is a brief roundup of the customer service concepts you have explored in this workbook. Check the items which you now feel more prepared to accomplish as a sales associate:

❏ Follow up with customers to make sure they are satisfied with their purchases

❏ Match your follow-up method and message to the individual customer

❏ Observe certain rules of etiquette when conducting customer follow-up

❏ Recognize when follow-up is warranted and when it is not

❏ Use business cards to build a relationship between you and your customer

❏ Create your own business card that tells customers you are a professional

❏ Create a client record

❏ Keep client information confidential

❏ Offer personal shopper services and be prepared to select options that meet customer needs

If you were unable to check one or more of the items listed above, review the pages related to those topics. You may want to practice some of these techniques and ideas on your friends and family to build your confidence and prepare you for going that extra mile with your customers.

Learning Checklist for Workbook 4

As you complete the workbook *Go the Extra Mile,* record your progress on this checklist. This checklist can also be used as a basis for discussion with your instructor, supervisor, or mentor as you complete the skill practices and/or you demonstrate the specific skills in the workplace.

Lessons completed	Date completed
❑ Conduct Customer Follow-up	_____
❑ Use Business Cards Artfully	_____
❑ Use Business Cards Artfully (continued)	_____
❑ Maintain Key Information on Customers	_____
❑ Offer Personal Shopper Services	_____

Skills Demonstrated in the Workplace	**Date Demonstrated**

❑ Conduct customer follow-up   _____

Describe the situation and how you demonstrated this skill:

_____

_____

_____

❑ Provide the customer with a personalized business card   _____

Describe the situation and how you demonstrated this skill:

_____

_____

_____

❑ Maintain key information on customers   _____

Describe the situation and how you demonstrated this skill:

_____

_____

_____

❑ Schedule personal appointments with shoppers; select merchandise in advance   _____

Describe the situation and how you demonstrated this skill:

_____

_____

_____

Appendix to Part 1

Comments & Suggested Responses

When to Follow Up

Your ideas may be somewhat different from the suggestions here, based on your own experiences and perspective. The important thing is to match your follow-up technique with the needs and preferences of each customer.

SITUATION	FOLLOW-UP
Your customer comes in every few months to see if you have any new neckties from his favorite designer.	Write him a note to let him know that you are expecting a new shipment in a week. Offer to hold some for him if he calls you with color preferences.
1. Your customer has purchased an entertainment center and asked to have it delivered and set up in her home.	Call to see if the furniture was delivered on time and assembled to her satisfaction. Ask if she was happy with the service. Thank her again for her business.
2. A customer recently returned a golf bag because it did not have all the features he wanted. You have just found one in your catalog that might fit his needs.	Send him the catalog (or a copy of the product information and a picture) with a note that says you thought of him when you saw this item. Offer to order one for him if he is interested.
3. The customer has been waiting for some specific new books to become available. They have finally arrived.	Call the customer to let her know the books are now available. Offer to have them delivered directly to her home or put them on hold for her if she'd prefer.
4. A customer has been in several times to look at wallpaper and has taken samples home but can't decide. You just found out one of your suppliers is sponsoring a wallpaper clinic, to be conducted by a noted decorator.	Send the customer a flyer about the clinic with a handwritten note that says the decorator may be able to help her with her wallpaper decisions. Suggest that you can reserve her a place in the clinic and ask her to call you if she is interested.

Appendix to Part 3

Comments & Suggested Responses

The Art of the Card Exchange

Only the examples which are checked (✓) follow the proper etiquette for requesting or offering business cards.

☑ **Sales Associate:** "I've enjoyed helping you select a wedding gift for your nephew, Mrs. Allen. Here is my business card in case I can be of any further assistance. Feel free to call me directly if you have any questions or special requests. Thank you, and enjoy the wedding!"

☐ **Sales Associate:** "Well, if you change your mind and do want some help, here's my card. Just tell the other sales people that I am already helping you."

☐ **Sales Associate:** "I'm glad I was able to help you find what you needed today. Here are a few of my cards—be sure and tell your friends and family about me."

☐ **Sales Associate:** "I'm sorry we don't carry that brand, but I think you'd be just as happy with the new model we have on order. If you have a business card, I could call you when it comes in."

☑ **Sales Associate:** "I agree you should give this some more thought if it is not exactly what you had in mind. Here is my card in case you think of any additional questions. In the meantime, if you'd like for me to keep an eye out as we get new shipments, I'd be happy to take your number and call you if I spot anything closer to your description."

☐ **Sales Associate:** "We don't have business cards here, but if you'll give me yours I will call you whenever something interesting comes in."

☑ **Sales Associate:** "I'm sorry I don't have a personalized business card to give you, but I've put my name, phone number, and the hours you can reach me on your sales slip—don't hesitate to call me if you have any questions about your new purchase."

confidential

Client Profile

Name: _____

Address: _____ Phone: _____

City/State/Zip: _____ Birthday: _____

Work: _____ Title: _____

Email: _____ Fax: _____

Contact Restrictions/Requests: _____

_____

Personal Profile (preferences, sizes, etc.): _____

_____

_____

_____

_____

Buying History: _____

_____

_____

_____

_____

_____

Recent Requests/Status: _____

_____

_____

_____

_____

_____

confidential

Client Profile

Name: _____

Address: _____ Phone: _____

City/State/Zip: _____ Birthday: _____

Work: _____ Title: _____

Email: _____ Fax: _____

Contact Restrictions/Requests: _____

_____

Personal Profile (preferences, sizes, etc.): _____

_____

_____

_____

_____

Buying History: _____

_____

_____

_____

_____

_____

Recent Requests/Status: _____

_____

_____

_____

_____

_____

---

confidential
Client Profile

Name: _____

Address: _____ Phone: _____

City/State/Zip: _____ Birthday: _____

Work: _____ Title: _____

Email: _____ Fax: _____

Contact Restrictions/Requests: _____

_____

Personal Profile (preferences, sizes, etc.): _____

_____

_____

_____

_____

Buying History: _____

_____

_____

_____

_____

_____

Recent Requests/Status: _____

_____

_____

_____

_____

_____

confidential

Client Profile

Name: _____

Address: _____ Phone: _____

City/State/Zip: _____ Birthday: _____

Work: _____ Title: _____

Email: _____ Fax: _____

Contact Restrictions/Requests: _____
_____

Personal Profile (preferences, sizes, etc.): _____
_____
_____
_____
_____

Buying History: _____
_____
_____
_____
_____
_____

Recent Requests/Status: _____
_____
_____
_____
_____
_____

confidential

Client Profile

Name: _____

Address: _____ Phone: _____

City/State/Zip: _____ Birthday: _____

Work: _____ Title: _____

Email: _____ Fax: _____

Contact Restrictions/Requests: _____

_____

Personal Profile (preferences, sizes, etc.): _____

_____

_____

_____

_____

Buying History: _____

_____

_____

_____

_____

_____

Recent Requests/Status: _____

_____

_____

_____

_____

_____

confidential

Client Profile

Name: _____

Address: _____ Phone: _____

City/State/Zip: _____ Birthday: _____

Work: _____ Title: _____

Email: _____ Fax: _____

Contact Restrictions/Requests: _____

_____

Personal Profile (preferences, sizes, etc.): _____

_____

_____

_____

_____

Buying History: _____

_____

_____

_____

_____

_____

Recent Requests/Status: _____

_____

_____

_____

_____

_____

---

confidential

Client Profile

Name: _____

Address: _____ Phone: _____

City/State/Zip: _____ Birthday: _____

Work: _____ Title: _____

Email: _____ Fax: _____

Contact Restrictions/Requests: _____

Personal Profile (preferences, sizes, etc.): _____

_____

_____

_____

_____

Buying History: _____

_____

_____

_____

_____

_____

Recent Requests/Status: _____

_____

_____

_____

_____

_____

.